AFRICAN ANIMALS ABC

PHILIPPA-ALYS BROWNE

BAREFOOT BOOKS

BATH

Antbear naps

Bushbaby blinks

Crocodile snaps

Dassie drinks

Elephant lumbers

Frog leaps

Giraffe dozes

Hippo sleeps

Impala grazes

Jackal prowls

Kingfisher dives

Lion growls

Monkey chatters

Nyala shivers

Ostrich dances

Porcupine quivers

Quail scuttles

Rhino stomps

Secretary bird stretches

Tortoise chomps

Umhutu hums

Vulture mutters

Warthog charges

Xoona moth flutters

Yellow-billed kite soars in the sky

Zebra watches the world go by

ANIMAL NOTES

Here are some facts about each of the animals in the pictures. At the beginning of each description the size of the animal illustrated is given; the length includes the tail measurement and the height is generally measured from the shoulder down.

In some cases the name of the animal is followed by 'endangered', 'specially protected' or 'vulnerable' written in brackets. 'Endangered' means that the species of animal is in danger of extinction and is unlikely to survive if the present factors for its decline continue. 'Vulnerable' indicates a species that may become endangered if the reasons for its decline continue. Being 'specially protected' will help to prevent a vulnerable species from becoming endangered, or an endangered species from becoming extinct.

ANTBEAR (*vulnerable*)

1,5 m long. This nocturnal mammal occurs throughout Africa, south of the Sahara. The antbear lives alone and during the day it can be found sleeping in its burrow in the ground. It eats mainly ants and termites, which it digs for and licks out of an ant nest or termite mound. Its tongue can extend to 30 cm. The antbear gives birth to a single offspring during the months of May to August.

BUSHBABY

70 cm long. There are four species of bushbaby, all found in Africa south of the Sahara. The thick-tailed bushbaby (shown in the picture) occurs in east and southern Africa. Bushbabies are primates that generally inhabit woodland, plantations and forests, where they feed off fruit, seeds, leaves, insects and smaller vertebrates. They are nocturnal, live alone and can leap great distances from tree to tree. At night bushbabies can be heard making loud child-like screams. Up to two young are born at a time during the months from August to November.

CROCODILE (*vulnerable*)

Up to 4 m long. The crocodile is a reptile that lives in the warmer parts of Africa, Asia, Australia and America. The picture shows a Nile crocodile, which used to occur throughout Africa, but due to hunting it has disappeared from central and north Africa. To maintain their body temperature crocodiles spend the day basking in the sun by rivers. They return to the water at midday, when it is too hot on the land, and in the evening when the land cools down. They feed off a variety of matter, from weed to insects, fish and even other crocodiles. Eggs are laid during the dry season and hatch four months later during the rainy season, which brings insects for the babies to live off.

DASSIE*

50 cm long. The dassie is a mammal that, although only the size of a rabbit, is considered to be the nearest relative to the elephant. The rock dassie can be found all over Africa, living in rocky hills and among areas of boulders at altitudes of up to 6,000ft. Dassies live in groups and use their acute eyesight and hearing to help them to escape from danger. When they are threatened, a few individuals in the group will give a warning bark or whistle. They feed for short periods in the mornings and evenings, and eat a mainly vegetarian diet, ranging from fruit to tree bark and twigs. Female dassies produce 2–3 offspring towards the end of the summer, after a gestation period of seven months.
*Dassie: 'rock hyrax' in Afrikaans (South African language).

ELEPHANT (*endangered**)

Up to 4 m high. The elephant is a mammal and the largest living land animal. The African elephant (shown in the picture) is the biggest species of elephant. It can be found all over Africa south of the Sahara, and lives in a variety of places, from savanna woodland to forest areas. Elephants live in groups, forming bigger herds of 'cows' and young or smaller groups of young 'bulls'. Old bulls often live alone. An elephant needs a great deal of food because of its size and rather ineffective digestive system. A typical elephant diet consists of bark, pods, leaves, fruit and other vegetable matter. Cows usually give birth during the rainy season, producing one offspring after a gestation period of twenty-four months.
*Its existence is not threatened in southern Africa, but it is regarded as endangered on the whole continent.

FROG

8,5 cm long. Tree frogs can be found throughout Africa. Like all frogs, they are amphibians. They mainly live in trees but a few live in water and some burrow in the ground. The foam nest tree frog (shown in the picture) lives in trees in woodland from northern Natal to Swaziland, Mozambique, Botswana and Zimbabwe. This frog changes colour from dark to light to suit its surroundings. It has clingy suckers at the ends of its toes to help it climb, and it catches a variety of insects. Up to 150 eggs are laid during the rainy season in a foamy nest in a tree above water. When ready, the eggs hatch as tadpoles and burst out of the foam, falling into the water below.

GIRAFFE

Up to 5,5 m high. Giraffes can be found from southern Africa up to Sudan and Ethiopia, and west to Senegal. They live in small herds, although the old 'bulls' often live alone. These tall mammals browse on the shoots and twigs of mainly acacia trees, but occasionally they can be seen grazing. Their sense of smell, sight and hearing is acute and they can ward off predators with a kick or a butt from the head. Calves are produced throughout the year, one per female being born after a gestation period of fifteen months.

HIPPOPOTAMUS

Up to 1,4 m high. The hippopotamus is a mammal, distantly related to the pig. Unlike the pygmy hippopotamus, the common hippo (shown in the picture) can be found throughout Africa. Hippos live in or by large rivers or swampy areas with reed beds. 'Schools' of up to twenty can be seen, although adult males often live alone. They are largely nocturnal, and graze upon vast amounts of vegetable matter at night, often several kilometres away from water. During the day they sleep partially submerged, with usually their heads and backs sticking out of the water. Hippos breed at any time of the year, normally producing one young at a time after a gestation period of eight months.

IMPALA

90 cm high. Impala are a type of antelope that can be found browsing or grazing in savanna throughout southern Africa up to Kenya and Uganda, and across to Namibia and Angola. They live in herds consisting of 'ewes' and young and a single dominant male. Bachelor herds are found separately. When startled, impala snort and dash off with their tails raised in the air like white flags. Their peak breeding period is between September and January, and one young is produced per female after a gestation period of 6–7 months.

JACKAL

Up to 40 cm high. The jackal is a fox-like creature. The black-backed jackal (shown in the picture) can be found in many areas of Africa, in light woodland or on the open plain. Jackals are mostly nocturnal and live alone or in pairs, although occasionally they appear in a family group. Their diet ranges from fruit to rats, mice, reptiles and birds. Jackal litters are generally six or more in size, and the young are born just after the rainy season.

KINGFISHER

45 cm long. Kingfishers are short-legged birds with dagger-like bills that occur in many parts of the world. The giant kingfisher (shown in the picture) can be found in all areas of Africa south of the Sahara, except the dry western parts. These alert birds live near wooded streams, dams and coastal lagoons, since their main food is fish. They occur singly or in pairs and are often to be seen perched on branches, bridges or along a wire fence as they watch for activity in the water. The giant kingfisher breeds in holes in the river bank or in trees from September to January.

LION

Up to 95 cm high. Lions can be found from the former South African province of the Transvaal to parts of Zululand and north to the Sahara. These large cats live in all types of countryside except forest, and occur singly, in pairs or family parties of up to ten. They hunt both day and night, usually seeking larger mammals as their prey. Lions breed throughout the year. The females leave the pride to give birth, producing 3–4 cubs per litter after a gestation period of 12–14 weeks.

MONKEY

1,2 m long. The vervet monkey (shown in the picture) is a primate that can be found all over Africa, from the Cape to northern Egypt. These creatures live in troops numbering up to twenty and can be found in woodland, bush savanna and riverine or montane forests. They are ususally omnivorous but tend more to a vegetarian diet of fruit, berries, leaves and roots. Most births appear to take place in the second half of the year and most are single. The baby can often be seen hanging from under the mother's belly or carried in her arms.

NYALA

1 m high. Nyala are a type of antelope that occur in southern Africa. They can be found grazing or browsing in riverine or other types of forest. They are generally nocturnal and occur singly or in pairs. When startled, nyala make a barking sound. They can be dangerous when wounded. Most young are born from August to October. A single offspring is produced per female, after a gestation period of 8–9 months.

OSTRICH

Up to 2 m high. This flightless bird occurs in isolated pockets throughout southern Africa, in areas ranging from woodland to grassland, thornveld and more arid regions. They eat succulents and other plants, but swallow stones to help with their digestion. The ostrich can run extremely fast – up to 60 kilometres per hour. When the male is excited, it often engorges its throat with air to make a lion-like roar. Each male bird mates with three females, who each lay 3–8 eggs into the same shallow hole, making a clutch of 15–20 eggs in total. Both the male and female birds take turns to incubate them.

PORCUPINE

80 cm long. The southern African crested porcupine (shown in the picture) may be found in any type of countryside from South Africa to Tanzania. This rodent is largely nocturnal, occurring singly, in pairs or in family groups, and makes a grunting, snuffling noise like a pig. It spends the day in caves or holes that it or another type of animal has dug. The porcupine's diet is vegetarian on the whole. When provoked, it will shake its quills and back on to its attacker, releasing quills like sharp arrows. The porcupine produces 1–3 young at any time from July to December, after a gestation period of about ten weeks.

QUAIL

18 cm long. There are nearly 100 species of quails throughout the world. The harlequin quail (shown in the picture) is to be found in pairs and lives in the bush, on grassland, pasture and cultivated fields. These birds are nomadic, terrestrial and feed off mainly seeds, shoots and insects. When disturbed, they can give out a piercing 'alarm' cry. The harlequin quail nests from August to October, and even as late as March, laying up to twelve eggs at a time.

RHINOCEROS (*endangered/specially protected*)

1,6 m high. (A square-lipped white rhinoceros is shown in the picture.) White and black rhinos, once found all over Africa, are now confined to highly protected pockets south of the Sahara. The white rhinoceros generally grazes during the cooler times of the day, and occurs singly, in pairs or family groups. It is often found in areas of dense and thorny bush. Rhinos have poor eyesight but a keen sense of smell, and communicate with each other in grunting, snorting and squealing noises. A single calf is produced every three years or so, after a gestation period of about 18 months, and in this species the baby usually walks ahead of its mother.

SECRETARY BIRD (*vulnerable/specially protected*)

1,25 m high. These large terrestrial birds generally occur in pairs and can be seen walking through grassland, bush or thornveld in areas south of the Sahara. When flying they may soar at a great height and, on landing, run a short distance with outspread wings. Secretary birds feed off insects, snakes, tortoises, young birds and any small animal that they can kill. They attack snakes using violent blows from their feet and holding out their wings as a shield. They roost at the top of thorn trees, and when disturbed they can be heard to make a frog-like croak. Secretary birds nest in a large platform of sticks which they lay below the top of a small tree. Breeding occurs from December to March, each female producing 2–3 eggs.

TORTOISE

Up to 30 cm high. (A hinged tortoise is shown in the picture.) This hard-shelled reptile is adapted to live in a variety of regions, from semi-arid countryside to riverine forest. It can be found in central and eastern regions of South Africa, as well as Mozambique, Zimbabwe and northern Botswana. During the day the hinged tortoise feeds off small insects and vegetable matter, and in the evening it can be seen settling in for the night. It rests in a shallow hole in a protected place such as a rocky over-hang or a termite mound. Its shell provides it with an armour-like protective layer as well as good camouflage. The female lays 1–5 eggs a year, mainly from March to April.

UMHUTU*

About 3 mm long. The umhutu, or mosquito, is an insect. Various species of this insect can carry diseases such as malaria and yellow fever. The common household mosquito (shown in the picture) can be found throughout Africa. It will breed in almost any stretch of stagnant water, laying a large number of eggs. These hatch into larvae, which become adult mosquitoes in about 2–3 weeks. It is only the female mosquito that sucks blood; the male lives on flower nectar and the juices of ripe fruit.

Umhutu: 'mosquito' in Shona (the language spoken by the Mashona tribe of Zimbabwe).

VULTURE (*vulnerable/specially protected*)

98 cm high. Vultures are scavengers, and can be found on other continents besides Africa. The lappet-faced vulture (shown in the picture) occurs throughout the area north of the former Cape Province of South Africa, up to Cairo and across to west Africa. These birds can be found in pairs in bushland, thornveld or desert. They feed on the flesh of dead animals and spend much of their day soaring in the sky searching for food. Normally they make no noise, but when squabbling over food they hiss and squeal. Vultures generally lay only one egg in a nest made of sticks in a tree or on a rocky ledge during June–August.

WARTHOG

Up to 75 cm high. This pig-like creature is widespread in Africa, usually occurring in grassland where there are some trees and bushes to give cover. Warthogs are found singly or in family groups, and during the heat of the day they can often be discovered sleeping. In the cool of the evening they forage for roots and fruit. When disturbed, the warthog can be seen dashing through the bush with its tail held erect like a beacon. Farrowing occurs from October to March, when up to six young are produced after a gestation period of about 18 weeks.

XOONA* MOTH

Up to 6 cm wide. A moth is a flying insect that is active mainly at night. The cream-striped owl moth (shown in the picture) is common throughout Africa south of the Sahara. It is generally nocturnal and often invades houses at night. It is attracted to rotting fruit, sweet and even alcoholic drinks. This moth lays thousands of eggs, which hatch into smooth larvae that feed on acacia trees.

Xoona: 'owl' in Tsonga (the language of the Tsonga tribe of Mozambique).

YELLOW-BILLED KITE

55 cm long. Kites are large, long-winged birds of prey with V-shaped tails. The yellow-billed kite (shown in the picture) is found all over Africa. This bird spends most of the day flying low in a leisurely manner, looking for prey – generally small animals such as mice, rats, snakes and other birds. The kite's nest consists of a platform of sticks laid in a tree. Often this is lined with dung, rags and wool. The breeding period is from September to December, and each female lays 2–3 eggs.

ZEBRA

Up to 1,3 m high. All species of this horse-like animal can be found in Africa. The Burchell's zebra (shown in the picture) occurs from South Africa to Sudan, Ethiopia and Somalia. Zebras are generally to be seen in tree- and bush-dotted grassland. They roam in large herds, often with wildebeest, roan, impala and ostriches. They neigh like horses but make a high-pitched bark or squeal when fighting. Zebras produce offspring throughout the year (each female giving birth to one foal), but the peak breeding season is July and August.